EASY QUICHE COOKBOOK

50 AMAZINGLY DELICIOUS QUICHE RECIPES

2ND EDITION

By
Chef Maggie Chow

Published by
BookSumo, a division of Saxonberg Associates
http://www.booksumo.com/

STAY TO THE END OF THE COOKBOOK AND RECEIVE....

I really appreciate when people, take the time to read all of my recipes.

So, as a gift for reading this entire cookbook you will receive a **massive collection of special recipes.**

Read to the end of this cookbook and get my ***Easy Specialty Cookbook Box Set for FREE***!

This box set includes the following:

1. ***Easy Sushi Cookbook***

2. ***Easy Dump Dinner Cookbook***
3. ***Easy Beans Cookbook***

Remember this box set is about **EASY** cooking.

In the ***Easy Sushi Cookbook*** you will learn the easiest methods to prepare almost every type of Japanese Sushi i.e. *California Rolls, the Perfect Sushi Rice, Crab Rolls, Osaka Style Sushi*, and so many others.

Then we go on to *Dump Dinners.* Nothing can be easier than a Dump Dinner. In the ***Easy Dump Dinner Cookbook*** we will learn how to master our slow cookers and make some amazingly unique dinners that will take almost ***no effort***.

Finally in the ***Easy Beans Cookbook*** we tackle one of my favorite side dishes: Beans. There are so many delicious ways to make Baked Beans and Bean Salads that I had to share them.

So stay till the end and then keep on cooking with my ***Easy Specialty Cookbook Box Set***!

About the Author.

Maggie Chow is the author and creator of your favorite *Easy Cookbooks* and *The Effortless Chef Series*. Maggie is a lover of all things related to food. Maggie loves nothing more than finding new recipes, trying them out, and then making them her own, by adding or removing ingredients, tweaking cooking times, and anything to make the recipe not only taste better, but be easier to cook!

For a complete listing of all my books please see my author page.

INTRODUCTION

Welcome to *The Effortless Chef Series*! Thank you for taking the time to download the *Easy Quiche Cookbook*. Come take a journey with me into the delights of easy cooking. The point of this cookbook and all my cookbooks is to exemplify the effortless nature of cooking simply.

In this book we focus on quiches. You will find that even though the recipes are simple, the taste of the dishes is quite amazing.

So will you join me in an adventure of simple cooking? If the answer is yes (and I hope it is) please consult the table of contents to find the dishes you are most interested in. Once you are ready jump right in and start cooking.

— Chef Maggie Chow

TABLE OF CONTENTS

Legal Notes

Chapter 1: Easy Quiche Recipes

The "Perfect" Quiche Crust

Ingredients

- 3/4 cup all-purpose flour
- 6 tbsps cold butter, cut into small pieces
- 1/4 cup shredded Cheddar cheese
- 5 tsps cold water

Directions

- Preheat your oven at 350 degrees F and put some oil over the quiche dish.
- Combine flour and butter in a bowl very thoroughly before adding grated cheese.
- Add water spoon after spoon until you can form a ball out of it.

- Wrap this dough with plastic wrap before refrigerating it for at least thirty minutes.
- Roll this dough and put this in the quiche dish.
- Bake in the preheated oven for about 10 minutes before filling it with quiche custard of your choice.

Serving: 6

Timing Information:

Preparation	Cooking	Total Time
10 mins	10 mins	20 mins

Nutritional Information:

Calories	178 kcal
Carbohydrates	12 g
Cholesterol	35 mg
Fat	13.2 g
Fiber	0.4 g
Protein	2.9 g
Sodium	111 mg

* Percent Daily Values are based on a 2,000 calorie diet.

AUTUMN ACORN QUICHE

Ingredients

- 2 acorn squash
- 1 red onion, chopped
- 1 cup chopped cooked turkey
- 4 eggs
- 1 tbsp pumpkin pie spice
- salt to taste

Directions

- Preheat your oven at 350 degrees F and put some oil over the quiche dish.
- Put squash into a baking dish and then bake it in the preheated oven for one full hour before cutting this in half, removing seeds and scrapping the meat out in a bowl.
- Combine squash, turkey, eggs, pumpkin pie spice, onion and salt together in a medium sized bowl

before pouring this mixture into the quiche dish

- Bake in the preheated oven for about 45 minutes or until the top of the quiche is golden brown in color.

Serving: 6

Timing Information:

Preparation	Cooking	Total Time
15 mins	1 hr 20 mins	1 hr 30 mins

Nutritional Information:

Calories	165 kcal
Carbohydrates	20 g
Cholesterol	142 mg
Fat	4.8 g
Fiber	2.9 g
Protein	12.6 g
Sodium	69 mg

* Percent Daily Values are based on a 2,000 calorie diet.

Veggie Cheese Bites

Ingredients

- 1/4 cup butter
- 2 (10 ounce) packages frozen broccoli florets, thawed and drained
- 1 pound shredded sharp Cheddar cheese
- 1 cup milk
- 1 cup all-purpose flour
- 3 eggs
- 1 tsp baking powder
- 1 tsp salt
- ground black pepper to taste

Directions

- Preheat your oven at 350 degrees F and put some oil over the quiche dish.
- Combine broccoli, milk, flour, eggs, baking powder, salt, Cheddar cheese and black pepper in medium sized bowl.

- Pour this mixture in the quiche dish over melted butter.
- Bake in the preheated oven for about 45 minutes or until the top of the quiche is golden brown in color.
- Serve.

Serving: 6

Timing Information:

Preparation	Cooking	Total Time
15 mins	45 mins	1 hr

Nutritional Information:

Calories	530 kcal
Carbohydrates	23.8 g
Cholesterol	196 mg
Fat	36.5 g
Fiber	3.4 g
Protein	28.2 g
Sodium	1068 mg

* Percent Daily Values are based on a 2,000 calorie diet.

Classical Baked Pear Dessert

Ingredients

- 4 Bosc pears
- 2 tbsps honey
- 3 tbsps butter, melted
- dash ground ginger

Directions

- Preheat your oven at 375 degrees F and put some oil over the quiche dish.
- Peel and cut a portion off of the bottom of your pears so that they can stand straight, and place them in the baking dish.
- Pour melted butter, honey and some ground ginger over these pears before covering the dish with aluminum foil.
- Bake in the preheated oven for about one hour or until the top is golden brown in color.

Serving: 4

Timing Information:

Preparation	Cooking	Total Time
15 mins	1 hr	1 hr 30 mins

Nutritional Information:

Calories	206 kcal
Carbohydrates	34.5 g
Cholesterol	23 mg
Fat	8.9 g
Fiber	5.2 g
Protein	0.8 g
Sodium	64 mg

* Percent Daily Values are based on a 2,000 calorie diet.

Ham and Cheese Quiche I

Ingredients

- 2 (12 ounce) packages frozen country style shredded hash brown potatoes
- 1/3 cup butter, melted
- 1/2 cup heavy whipping cream
- 2 eggs
- 1 cup diced cooked ham
- 1 cup shredded Monterey Jack and Cheddar cheese blend

Directions

- Preheat your oven at 425 degrees F and put some oil over the quiche dish.
- Put a mixture of potatoes and butter in the quiche dish as a crust.
- Bake this in the preheated oven for about 25 minutes.

- Combine cream and eggs in a bowl before mixing it with the potatoes in a bowl.
- Form a layer of ham and Monterey Jack cheese in the quiche dish before pouring this mixture over it.
- Bake in the preheated oven for about 30 minutes or until the top of the quiche is golden brown in color.

Serving: 10

Timing Information:

Preparation	Cooking	Total Time
15 mins	55 mins	1 hr 10 mins

Nutritional Information:

Calories	286 kcal
Carbohydrates	15.6 g
Cholesterol	110 mg
Fat	25.2 g
Fiber	1.2 g
Protein	11 g
Sodium	422 mg

* Percent Daily Values are based on a 2,000 calorie diet.

Ham and Cheese Quiche II (Low Cholesterol)

Ingredients

- 1 prepared 9-inch single pie crust
- 1 tbsp olive oil
- 4 green onions, chopped
- 1/2 pound cooked ham, cubed
- 1 cup fat-free egg substitute
- 7 fluid ounces fat-free evaporated milk
- 1/4 cup shredded part-skim mozzarella cheese
- 1 tbsp grated Parmesan cheese
- 1 tsp chopped fresh chives (optional)

Directions

- Preheat your oven at 325 degrees F and put some oil over the quiche dish before pressing pie crust into it.

- Cook green onions in hot oil for about 3 minutes before adding this on top of ham that is spread on the pie crust.
- Pour a mixture of mozzarella cheese, egg substitute and evaporated milk over the ham mixture before adding Parmesan cheese and chives.
- Bake in the preheated oven for about 20 minutes before turning the heat up to 350 Degrees F and baking for another 20 minutes or until the top of the quiche is golden brown in color.
- Allow it to set for thirty minutes before serving.

Serving: 8

Timing Information:

Preparation	Cooking	Total Time
15 mins	35 mins	1 hr 20 mins

Nutritional Information:

Calories	261 kcal
Carbohydrates	14.3 g
Cholesterol	20 mg
Fat	16.3 g
Fiber	1 g
Protein	13.7 g
Sodium	602 mg

* Percent Daily Values are based on a 2,000 calorie diet.

A Quiche Of Mushrooms and Spinach

Ingredients

- 6 slices bacon
- 4 eggs, beaten
- 1 1/2 cups light cream
- 1/4 tsp ground nutmeg
- 1/2 tsp salt
- 1/2 tsp pepper
- 2 cups chopped fresh spinach
- 2 cups chopped fresh mushrooms
- 1/2 cup chopped onions
- 1 cup shredded Swiss cheese
- 1 cup shredded Cheddar cheese
- 1 (9 inch) deep dish pie crust

Directions

- Preheat your oven at 400 degrees F and put some oil over the quiche dish.

- Cook bacon over medium heat until brown and then crumble it after draining.
- Mix eggs, pepper, cream, salt, nutmeg, bacon, spinach, mushrooms, 3/4 cup Swiss cheese, 3/4 cup Cheddar cheese and onions in a bowl very thoroughly.
- Pour this mixture over the pie crust and add some cheese.
- Bake in the preheated oven for about 35 minutes or until the top of the quiche is golden brown in color.

Serving: 9

Timing Information:

Preparation	Cooking	Total Time
15 mins	35 mins	50 mins

Nutritional Information:

Calories	325 kcal
Carbohydrates	10.8 g
Cholesterol	139 mg
Fat	22.5 g
Fiber	2.3 g
Protein	20.9 g
Sodium	806 mg

* Percent Daily Values are based on a 2,000 calorie diet.

The Simplest Zucchini Quiche I

Ingredients

- 2 cups grated zucchini
- 1 (9 inch) pie shell, unbaked
- 6 eggs, beaten
- 1 cup shredded Cheddar cheese

Directions

- Preheat your oven at 350 degrees F and put some oil over the quiche dish.
- Put zucchini evenly in quiche dish before adding eggs and some cheddar cheese.
- Bake in the preheated oven for about 30 minutes or until the top of the quiche is golden brown in color.

Serving: 9

Timing Information:

Preparation	Cooking	Total Time
15 mins	30 mins	45 mins

Nutritional Information:

Calories	314 kcal
Carbohydrates	15.7 g
Cholesterol	188 mg
Fat	22 g
Fiber	1.6 g
Protein	13.6 g
Sodium	364 mg

* Percent Daily Values are based on a 2,000 calorie diet.

A Quiche of Chili's and Spinach

Ingredients

- 1/2 cup all-purpose flour
- 1 tsp baking powder
- 1 tsp salt
- 12 eggs
- 1 (8 ounce) package shredded Colby-Monterey Jack cheese
- 2 cups small curd cottage cheese
- 1 (10 ounce) package frozen chopped spinach, thawed and drained
- 2 (4 ounce) cans chopped green chilies
- 1/2 cup melted butter
- 2 (9 inch) unbaked pie crusts

Directions

- Preheat your oven at 400 degrees F and put some oil over the quiche dish before setting aside a mixture of salt, flour and baking powder.

- Whisk eggs and flour mixture together thoroughly before adding Colby-Monterey Jack cheese, spinach, green chills, cottage cheese and melted butter into it.
- Pour this mixture evenly into the quiche dishes.
- Bake in the preheated oven for about 15 minutes before turning the heat down to 350 Degrees F and baking for another 40 minutes or until the top of the quiche is golden brown in color.

Serving: 18

Timing Information:

Preparation	Cooking	Total Time
10 mins	50 mins	1 hr

Nutritional Information:

Calories	324 kcal
Carbohydrates	16.3 g
Cholesterol	173 mg
Fat	22.9 g
Fiber	1.6 g
Protein	14 g
Sodium	786 mg

* Percent Daily Values are based on a 2,000 calorie diet.

Crab Quiche I

Ingredients

- 1/2 cup mayonnaise
- 2 tbsps all-purpose flour
- 2 eggs, beaten
- 1/2 cup milk
- 1 cup crab meat
- 1 cup diced Swiss cheese
- 1/2 cup chopped green onions
- 1 (9 inch) unbaked pie crust

Directions

- Preheat your oven at 350 degrees F and put some oil over the quiche dish.
- Whisk eggs, milk, mayonnaise, crab, flour, onion and cheese very thoroughly.
- Pour this mixture in the quiche dish.
- Bake in the preheated oven for about 30 minutes or until the top

of the quiche is golden brown in color.

Serving: 6

Timing Information:

Preparation	Cooking	Total Time
10 mins	45 mins	1 hr

Nutritional Information:

Calories	326 kcal
Carbohydrates	14.3 g
Cholesterol	83 mg
Fat	24.8 g
Fiber	1 g
Protein	11.8 g
Sodium	308 mg

* Percent Daily Values are based on a 2,000 calorie diet.

A QUICHE OF PARMESAN

Ingredients

- 2 cups milk
- 4 eggs
- 3/4 cup biscuit baking mix
- 1/4 cup butter, softened
- 1 cup grated Parmesan cheese
- 1 (10 ounce) package chopped frozen broccoli, thawed and drained
- 1 cup cubed cooked ham
- 8 ounces shredded Cheddar cheese

Directions

- Preheat your oven to 375 degrees F and put some oil over the quiche dish.
- Now mix milk, eggs, parmesan cheese, baking mix and some butter in a bowl and then add broccoli, cheddar cheese and ham.
- Mix thoroughly and bake in the preheated oven for about 50

minutes or until the top of the quiche is golden brown in color.

Serving: 10 inch pie

Timing Information:

Preparation	Cooking	Total Time
10 mins	50 mins	1 hr

Nutritional Information:

Calories	371 kcal
Carbohydrates	12.5 g
Cholesterol	161 mg
Fat	26.6 g
Fiber	1.3 g
Protein	21 g
Sodium	797 mg

* Percent Daily Values are based on a 2,000 calorie diet.

A QUICHE OF BACON AND SWISS

Ingredients

- 8 slices bacon
- 4 ounces shredded Swiss cheese
- 2 tbsps butter, melted
- 4 eggs, beaten
- 1/4 cup finely chopped onion
- 1 tsp salt
- 1/2 cup all-purpose flour
- 1 1/2 cups milk

Directions

- Preheat your oven to 375 degrees F and put some oil over the quiche dish.
- Cook bacon over medium heat until brown and then crumble.
- Put cheese and this crumbled bacon at the bottom of the dish and now mix milk, eggs, onion, salt and some butter in a bowl and add into the pan.
- Bake in the preheated oven for about 35 minutes or until the top

of the quiche is golden brown in color.

Serving: 6

Timing Information:

Preparation	Cooking	Total Time
15 mins	35 mins	50 mins

Nutritional Information:

Calories	291 kcal
Carbohydrates	12.9 g
Cholesterol	170 mg
Fat	18.8 g
Fiber	0.4 g
Protein	17 g
Sodium	804 mg

* Percent Daily Values are based on a 2,000 calorie diet.

Spinach Quiche

Ingredients

- 1 (10 ounce) package frozen chopped spinach, thawed
- 1 bunch green onions, finely chopped (white parts only)
- 4 eggs, beaten
- 1 (16 ounce) package cottage cheese
- 2 cups shredded Cheddar cheese
- 1/4 cup crushed croutons

Directions

- Preheat your oven to 375 degrees F and put some oil over the quiche dish.
- Cook spinach over medium heat until soft and now mix cheddar cheese, eggs, onion, salt and some cottage cheese in a bowl and pour this into the pan
- Mix it thoroughly and bake in the preheated oven for about one hour or until the top of the quiche is golden brown in color.

Serving: 8

Timing Information:

Preparation	Cooking	Total Time
10 mins	1 hr	1 hr 10 mins

Nutritional Information:

Calories	231 kcal
Carbohydrates	6.1 g
Cholesterol	131 mg
Fat	14.9 g
Fiber	1.8 g
Protein	19.1 g
Sodium	478 mg

* Percent Daily Values are based on a 2,000 calorie diet.

Crab Quiche II

Ingredients

- 1 (9 inch pie) deep dish frozen pie crust
- 4 eggs
- 1 cup heavy cream
- 1/2 tsp salt
- 1/2 tsp black pepper
- 3 dashes hot pepper sauce (e.g. Tabasco™), or to taste
- 1 cup shredded Monterey Jack cheese
- 1/4 cup grated Parmesan cheese
- 1 (8 ounce) package imitation crabmeat, flaked
- 1 green onion, chopped

Directions

- Preheat your oven to 375 degrees F and put some oil over the quiche dish.
- Bake pie crust for about 10 minutes to get it crispy
- Now mix shredded cheese, eggs, onion, salt, cream, pepper,

imitation crab and hot sauce in a bowl and pour this into baked pie.

- Bake in the preheated oven for about 30 minutes or until the top of the quiche is golden brown in color and an additional 30 minutes in the oven after turning it off.

Serving: 9 inch pie

Timing Information:

Preparation	Cooking	Total Time
10 mins	50 mins	1 hr

Nutritional Information:

Calories	346 kcal
Carbohydrates	16.9 g
Cholesterol	154 mg
Fat	26.1 g
Fiber	0.5 g
Protein	11.4 g
Sodium	691 mg

* Percent Daily Values are based on a 2,000 calorie diet.

A Classic Quiche

Ingredients

- 1 tbsp butter
- 1 large onion, diced
- 3 eggs
- 1/3 cup heavy cream
- 1/3 cup shredded Swiss cheese
- 1 (9 inch pie) unbaked pie crust

Directions

- Preheat your oven to 375 degrees F and put some oil over the quiche dish.
- Melt butter over medium heat and then cook onions in it until soft.
- Now whisk eggs and cream together in a bowl and then add cheese.
- Place onion at the bottom of the dish and pour this mixture over it.
- Bake in the preheated oven for about 30 minutes or until the top

of the quiche is golden brown in color.

Serving: 8

Timing Information:

Preparation	Cooking	Total Time
10 mins	30 mins	40 mins

Nutritional Information:

Calories	212 kcal
Carbohydrates	12.7 g
Cholesterol	91 mg
Fat	15.7 g
Fiber	1.1 g
Protein	5.4 g
Sodium	211 mg

* Percent Daily Values are based on a 2,000 calorie diet.

ZUCCHINI QUICHE

Ingredients

- 1 cup biscuit baking mix
- 1 tsp dried oregano
- 1 tsp seasoning salt
- 1/2 tsp garlic powder
- 1/4 tsp salt
- 1 tsp dried parsley
- 1/3 cup grated Parmesan cheese
- 1/2 cup grated onion
- 4 eggs, beaten
- 1/3 cup vegetable oil
- 1 zucchini, sliced into rounds

Directions

- Preheat your oven to 375 degrees F and put some oil over the quiche dish.
- Combine biscuit mix, seasoning salt, garlic powder, salt, oregano, parsley, Parmesan cheese, eggs and onion in a bowl.
- Now add zucchini and put this in the dish.

- Bake in the preheated oven for about 30 minutes or until the top of the quiche is golden brown in color.

Serving: 6

Timing Information:

Preparation	Cooking	Total Time
10 mins	35 mins	45 mins

Nutritional Information:

Calories	272 kcal
Carbohydrates	15.4 g
Cholesterol	129 mg
Fat	20.1 g
Fiber	1.2 g
Protein	8.4 g
Sodium	635 mg

* Percent Daily Values are based on a 2,000 calorie diet.

SEAFOOD QUICHE

Ingredients

- 6 ounces crabmeat
- 1/2 cup bread crumbs
- 1/2 cup milk
- 2 eggs, beaten
- 2 tbsps chopped fresh parsley
- 1 tbsp lemon juice
- 1 tsp prepared mustard
- 1/4 tsp Worcestershire sauce
- salt to taste
- ground black pepper to taste
- 1 pinch pie cayenne pepper
- 1 pinch pie paprika

Directions

- Preheat your oven to 400 degrees F and put some oil over the quiche dish.
- Remove any shells or cartilage that you may find from the crab meat.
- Combine all the ingredients except paprika which are mentioned; in a bowl and pour

this mixture into the prepared dish.

- Bake in the preheated oven for about 30 minutes or until the top of the quiche is golden brown in color.

Serving: 6

Timing Information:

Preparation	Cooking	Total Time
10 mins	30 mins	40 mins

Nutritional Information:

Calories	95 kcal
Carbohydrates	8.2 g
Cholesterol	80 mg
Fat	2.8 g
Fiber	0.5 g
Protein	8.9 g
Sodium	183 mg

* Percent Daily Values are based on a 2,000 calorie diet.

A Quiche of Swiss and Ham

Ingredients

- 1 sheet frozen puff pastry, thawed
- 1 cup milk
- 3 eggs
- 1/4 cup frozen chopped spinach, thawed and drained
- salt and ground black pepper to taste
- 1 cup shredded Swiss cheese
- 3/4 cup chopped cooked ham
- 1 small tomato, sliced (optional)

Directions

- Preheat your oven to 400 degrees F and put some oil over the quiche dish after putting some puff pastry at the bottom of the baking dish.
- Combine milk, salt, eggs and spinach in a bowl very thoroughly and pour this mixture over the puff after adding a cheese and ham layer.

- Bake in the preheated oven for about 30 minutes or until the top of the quiche is golden brown in color.

Serving: 4

Timing Information:

Preparation	Cooking	Total Time
10 mins	50 mins	1 hr

Nutritional Information:

Calories	611 kcal
Carbohydrates	33.4 g
Cholesterol	189 mg
Fat	41.8 g
Fiber	1.5 g
Protein	25.3 g
Sodium	663 mg

* Percent Daily Values are based on a 2,000 calorie diet.

ZUCCHINI QUICHE II

Ingredients

- 2 cups grated zucchini
- 1 (9 inch pie) pie shell, unbaked
- 6 eggs, beaten
- 1 cup shredded Cheddar cheese

Directions

- Preheat your oven to 400 degrees F and put some oil over the quiche dish.
- Put some zucchini at bottom of the dish and add eggs and some cheddar cheese over it.
- Bake in the preheated oven for about 30 minutes or until the top of the quiche is golden brown in color.

Serving: 9 inch pie

Timing Information:

Preparation	Cooking	Total Time
10 mins	50 mins	1 hr

Nutritional Information:

Calories	314 kcal
Carbohydrates	15.7 g
Cholesterol	188 mg
Fat	22 g
Fiber	1.6 g
Protein	13.6 g
Sodium	364 mg

* Percent Daily Values are based on a 2,000 calorie diet.

Zucchini Pie

Ingredients

- 1 (10 inch pie) unbaked pie crust
- 2 tbsps butter, melted
- 2/3 cup bacon bits
- 4 cups diced zucchini
- 4 eggs
- 1/2 cup heavy cream
- 1/2 tsp dried marjoram
- 1 tsp onion salt
- 1/4 tsp cayenne pepper
- 2 cups shredded Cheddar cheese

Directions

- Preheat your oven to 400 degrees F and put some oil over the quiche dish.
- Put some crumbled bacon in the dish and then blend cream, zucchini and eggs very thoroughly.
- Now add marjoram, cayenne, onion salt and this mix together.
- Also add some cheese and pour this into the dish.

- Bake in the preheated oven for about 30 minutes or until the top of the quiche is golden brown in color.

Serving: 8

Timing Information:

Preparation	Cooking	Total Time
10 mins	1 hr	1 hr 10 mins

Nutritional Information:

Calories	410 kcal
Carbohydrates	16.2 g
Cholesterol	157 mg
Fat	31.5 g
Fiber	1.9 g
Protein	16.6 g
Sodium	902 mg

* Percent Daily Values are based on a 2,000 calorie diet.

A Classic Quiche II

Ingredients

- 12 slices bread
- 1 onion, grated
- 1/2 cup shredded Swiss cheese
- 1 cup milk
- 4 eggs
- 1 tsp dry mustard
- 1 pinch pie black pepper

Directions

- Preheat your oven to 400 degrees F and put some oil over the muffin tins.
- Now cut some circles from the bread and put these circles into these muffins tin.
- Put shredded cheese and onion evenly in all the tins.
- Now add a mixture of milk, pepper, eggs and mustard into all the tins evenly.
- Bake in the preheated oven for about 30 minutes or until the top

of the quiche is golden brown in color.

Serving: 12

Timing Information:

Preparation	Cooking	Total Time
10 mins	20 mins	30 mins

Nutritional Information:

Calories	123 kcal
Carbohydrates	15 g
Cholesterol	68 mg
Fat	4.2 g
Fiber	0.8 g
Protein	6.1 g
Sodium	233 mg

* Percent Daily Values are based on a 2,000 calorie diet.

Ham and Cheese Quiche II

Ingredients

- 2 tbsps all-purpose flour
- 1/2 tsp salt
- 1 cup half-and-half
- 3 eggs
- 2 slices Swiss cheese
- 1 recipe pastry for a 9 inch pie single crust pie
- 1/2 cup chopped fresh spinach
- 1/2 cup canned mushrooms
- 1 (4.5 ounce) can ham, flaked
- 1/2 cup shredded Cheddar cheese

Directions

- Preheat your oven to 350 degrees F and put some oil over the quiche dish.
- Combine flour, eggs, salt and half-and-half in a bowl of medium size
- Put spinach over Swiss cheese in the baking dish and then add mushrooms.

- Pour the previous mixture into it and add flaked ham and some cheddar cheese over it
- Bake in the preheated oven for about 55 minutes or until the top of the quiche is golden brown in color.

Serving: 9 inch pie

Timing Information:

Preparation	Cooking	Total Time
15 mins	55 mins	1 hr 10 mins

Nutritional Information:

Calories	283 kcal
Carbohydrates	14.3 g
Cholesterol	103 mg
Fat	20.1 g
Fiber	1.2 g
Protein	11.3 g
Sodium	621 mg

* Percent Daily Values are based on a 2,000 calorie diet.

A Quiche of Bacon, Swiss, & Cheddar

Ingredients

- 1 (3 ounce) can bacon bits
- 1/2 cup chopped onion
- 5 ounces shredded Swiss cheese
- 3 ounces grated Cheddar cheese
- 1 (9 inch pie) deep dish frozen pie crust
- 4 eggs, lightly beaten
- 1 cup half-and-half cream

Directions

- Preheat your oven to 400 degrees F and put some oil over the quiche dish.
- Pour mixture of eggs and half-and-half over the mixture of both cheeses, bacon and onion in the dish.
- Bake in the preheated oven for about 15 minutes and then an additional 35 minutes at 350 degrees F or until the top of the quiche is golden brown in color.

Serving: 6

Timing Information:

Preparation	Cooking	Total Time
10 mins	50 mins	1 hr

Nutritional Information:

Calories	462 kcal
Carbohydrates	20.2 g
Cholesterol	183 mg
Fat	31.5 g
Fiber	0.5 g
Protein	24.7 g
Sodium	993 mg

* Percent Daily Values are based on a 2,000 calorie diet.

Broccoli and Cheddar Quiche

Ingredients

- 1 cup sliced fresh mushrooms
- 1 cup chopped onions
- 1 cup chopped broccoli
- 5 eggs
- 1/3 cup MIRACLE WHIP Calorie-Wise Dressing
- 1/3 cup milk
- 1 cup KRAFT Double Cheddar Shredded Cheese Light
- 1 frozen deep-dish pie crust (9 inch pie)

Directions

- Preheat your oven to 400 degrees F and put some oil over the quiche dish.
- Cook all the vegetables in hot oil over medium heat for about 5 minutes.
- Now add this mixture of vegetables and cheese into the

mixture of eggs, milk and dressing.

- Put this into the baking dish
- Bake in the preheated oven for about 45 minutes or until the top of the quiche is golden brown in color.

Serving: 8

Timing Information:

Preparation	Cooking	Total Time
10 mins		55 mins

Nutritional Information:

Calories	401 kcal
Carbohydrates	10.6 g
Cholesterol	202 mg
Fat	32.4 g
Fiber	2.5 g
Protein	19.3 g
Sodium	796 mg

* Percent Daily Values are based on a 2,000 calorie diet.

Spinach Muenster Quiche

Ingredients

- 8 ounces Muenster cheese, sliced
- 2 (10 ounce) packages frozen chopped spinach, thawed and drained
- 2 eggs
- 1/3 cup grated Parmesan cheese
- 1 (8 ounce) package cream cheese, softened
- salt and pepper to taste
- garlic powder to taste
- 4 ounces Muenster cheese, sliced

Directions

- Preheat your oven to 350 degrees F and put some oil over the quiche dish.
- Put Muenster cheese slices into the dish and then pour into it the mixture of spinach (all water drained), eggs, Parmesan cheese, cream cheese, salt, pepper and garlic powder.

- Bake in the preheated oven for about 30 minutes or until the top of the quiche is golden brown in color.

Serving: 8

Timing Information:

Preparation	Cooking	Total Time
10 mins	35 mins	45 mins

Nutritional Information:

Calories	311 kcal
Carbohydrates	4.5 g
Cholesterol	122 mg
Fat	25.4 g
Fiber	2.1 g
Protein	17.8 g
Sodium	484 mg

* Percent Daily Values are based on a 2,000 calorie diet.

Spinach and Ham Quiche

Ingredients

- 1 (10 ounce) package frozen chopped spinach, thawed and drained
- 1 1/2 cups milk
- 1 cup diced cooked ham
- 3 eggs, beaten
- 3/4 cup baking mix (such as Bisquick ®)
- 1/2 cup chopped onion
- 1/2 cup shredded sharp Cheddar cheese
- 1/2 cup shredded Monterey Jack cheese

Directions

- Preheat your oven to 350 degrees F and put some oil over the quiche dish.
- Make a layer of spinach over the dish and then pour mixture of milk, ham, baking mix, onion, eggs, Cheddar cheese, and Monterey Jack over this layer.

- Bake in the preheated oven for about 30 minutes or until the top of the quiche is golden brown in color.

Serving: 10 inch pie

Timing Information:

Preparation	Cooking	Total Time
15 mins	35 mins	50 mins

Nutritional Information:

Calories	275 kcal
Carbohydrates	15.7 g
Cholesterol	129 mg
Fat	16.4 g
Fiber	1.9 g
Protein	16.9 g
Sodium	682 mg

* Percent Daily Values are based on a 2,000 calorie diet.

Crab Quiche III

Ingredients

- 1 (9 inch pie) deep dish pie crust
- 2 eggs, beaten
- 1/2 cup milk
- 1/2 cup mayonnaise
- 1 tsp cornstarch
- 1 1/2 cups shredded Swiss cheese
- 1/2 pound imitation crabmeat
- 1 pinch pie ground black pepper

Directions

- Preheat your oven to 350 degrees F and put some oil over the quiche dish.
- Mix eggs, cornstarch, cheese, pepper, mayonnaise, milk and imitation crabmeat thoroughly.
- Pour this mixture into the baking dish.
- Bake in the preheated oven for about 30 minutes or until the top of the quiche is golden brown in color.

Serving: 8

Timing Information:

Preparation	Cooking	Total Time
5 mins	40 mins	45 mins

Nutritional Information:

Calories	396 kcal
Carbohydrates	20.9 g
Cholesterol	88 mg
Fat	29.4 g
Fiber	0.5 g
Protein	12.4 g
Sodium	602 mg

* Percent Daily Values are based on a 2,000 calorie diet.

VEGETABLE QUICHE CUPS

Ingredients

- cooking spray
- 1 (10 ounce) package frozen chopped spinach, thawed and drained
- 3/4 cup liquid egg substitute
- 3/4 cup shredded reduced-fat Cheddar cheese
- 1/4 cup diced onion
- 1/4 cup chopped green bell pepper
- 3 drops hot pepper sauce(optional)

Directions

- Preheat your oven to 350 degrees F and put some oil over the muffin tins.
- Combine all the ingredients mentioned above in a bowl and then divide it evenly among all the muffin tins.
- Bake in the preheated oven for about 20 minutes or until the top

of the quiche is golden brown in color.

Serving: 6

Timing Information:

Preparation	Cooking	Total Time
15 mins	20 mins	35 mins

Nutritional Information:

Calories	69 kcal
Carbohydrates	3.4 g
Cholesterol	3 mg
Fat	2.4 g
Fiber	1.6 g
Protein	9.1 g
Sodium	189 mg

* Percent Daily Values are based on a 2,000 calorie diet.

Crab and Cheddar Quiche

Ingredients

- 1 (9 inch pie) unbaked pie crust
- 3 eggs
- 1/2 cup mayonnaise
- 1/2 cup whole milk
- 2 tbsps all-purpose flour
- 1 tsp seafood seasoning (such as Old Bay®)
- 1 cup shredded Cheddar cheese
- 1/2 cup chopped fresh parsley
- 1 cup crabmeat
- 1 pinch pie seafood seasoning (such as Old Bay®), or to taste

Directions

- Preheat your oven to 350 degrees F and put some oil over the quiche dish.
- Whisk eggs, 1 tsp seafood seasoning, milk and flour thoroughly and then add some cheddar cheese and parsley.
- Fold crab meat in this mixture and pour it over the prepared

dish, and also add some seafood seasoning over it.

- Bake in the preheated oven for about 45 minutes or until the top of the quiche is golden brown in color.

Serving: 9 inch pie

Timing Information:

Preparation	Cooking	Total Time
15 mins	40 mins	55 mins

Nutritional Information:

Calories	333 kcal
Carbohydrates	13.7 g
Cholesterol	104 mg
Fat	25.7 g
Fiber	1.1 g
Protein	12 g
Sodium	453 mg

* Percent Daily Values are based on a 2,000 calorie diet.

AGRARIAN QUICHE

Ingredients

- 1 tbsp butter
- 1 large sweet onion (such as Vidalia®), cut into chunks
- 6 eggs
- 1/2 cup whole milk
- 10 ounces shredded Jarlsberg cheese
- 2 ounces freshly grated Parmesan cheese
- 2 bunches Swiss chard, stems and leaves separated
- 1 tsp fresh thyme leaves
- 1 pinch pie nutmeg
- salt and ground black pepper to taste
- 1 prepared 10-inch pie pie crust

Directions

- Preheat your oven to 375 degrees F and put some oil over the quiche dish.
- Cook onion in hot butter over medium heat for about 7 minutes

and then place it in a large sized bowl

- Blend parmesan cheese, eggs, milk and jarlsberg cheese in a blender until required smoothness is achieved and then add this into the bowl containing onion.
- Now add black pepper, nutmeg, salt and some thyme into it and mix it thoroughly before pouring this mixture into the baking dish.
- Bake in the preheated oven for about 45 minutes or until the top of the quiche is golden brown in color.

Serving: 10 inch pie

Timing Information:

Preparation	Cooking	Total Time
15 mins	50 mins	1 hr 5 mins

Nutritional Information:

Calories	506 kcal
Carbohydrates	29.7 g
Cholesterol	134 mg
Fat	34.1 g
Fiber	3.1 g
Protein	20.6 g
Sodium	627 mg

* Percent Daily Values are based on a 2,000 calorie diet.

QUICHE A LA MARTINIQUE

Ingredients

- 1 (9 inch pie) unbaked 9 inch pie pie crust
- 1/2 cup shredded Swiss cheese
- 1/2 onion, minced
- 1 (4.5 ounce) can sliced mushrooms, drained
- 3 egg yolks
- 2 egg whites
- 2 tbsps all-purpose flour
- 2 tbsps milk
- 1/2 tsp chopped fresh thyme
- salt and pepper to taste

Directions

- Preheat your oven to 350 degrees F and put some oil over the quiche dish.
- Make a layer of cheese, mushrooms and onions in the baking dish and pour mixture of eggs whites, milk, yolks and flour over it.

- Spread it evenly and then add thyme, pepper and some salt.
- Bake in the preheated oven for about 30 minutes or until the top of the quiche is golden brown in color.

Serving: 6

Timing Information:

Preparation	Cooking	Total Time
15 mins	30 mins	45 mins

Nutritional Information:

Calories	239 kcal
Carbohydrates	18.8 g
Cholesterol	111 mg
Fat	14.9 g
Fiber	1.8 g
Protein	7.8 g
Sodium	287 mg

* Percent Daily Values are based on a 2,000 calorie diet.

MINI QUICHE II

Ingredients

- 15 mini phyllo tart shells
- 1/2 cup shredded Swiss cheese
- 1/3 cup crumbled cooked bacon
- 1 egg
- 1/2 cup half-and-half
- 1/4 tsp dried basil
- 1/4 tsp dried parsley
- 1/4 tsp garlic powder
- 1/4 tsp salt
- 1/8 tsp ground black pepper

Directions

- Preheat your oven to 350 degrees F and put some oil over the quiche dish.
- Put phyllo tart shells in the baking dish and in each shell put one tsp of Swiss cheese and half a tsp of bacon
- Whisk egg, half-and-half, basil, parsley, garlic powder, salt, and black pepper lightly in a bowl and

put tsp of this mixture in each shell.

- Add contents to your baking dish.
- Bake in the preheated oven for about 15 minutes or until the top of the quiche is lightly brown in color.

Serving: 8

Timing Information:

Preparation	Cooking	Total Time
15 mins	15 mins	30 mins

Nutritional Information:

Calories	401 kcal
Carbohydrates	10.6 g
Cholesterol	202 mg
Fat	32.4 g
Fiber	2.5 g
Protein	19.3 g
Sodium	796 mg

* Percent Daily Values are based on a 2,000 calorie diet.

A Quiche Without A Crust

Ingredients

- 4 eggs
- 1 (16 ounce) container sour cream
- 1 (10 ounce) package frozen chopped spinach, thawed and drained
- 1 cup shredded Cheddar cheese
- 1/2 cup crumbled feta cheese
- 1/2 cup shredded Parmesan cheese
- 1/2 cup chopped onion
- 1/2 cup chopped tomato
- 1 (4 ounce) can canned chopped green chiles, drained
- 1 tsp minced garlic
- 1 tsp ground cumin
- 1 tbsp paprika
- 1/4 tsp cayenne pepper

Directions

- Preheat your oven to 325 degrees F and put some oil over the quiche dish.

- Whisk eggs and sour cream in a bowl until smooth and then add all the remaining ingredients into this bowl.
- Mix everything thoroughly and then place contents into your baking dish.
- Bake in the preheated oven for about 1 hour or until the top of the quiche is golden brown in color.

Serving: 6

Timing Information:

Preparation	Cooking	Total Time
15 mins	1 hr	1 hr 15 mins

Nutritional Information:

Calories	401 kcal
Carbohydrates	10.6 g
Cholesterol	202 mg
Fat	32.4 g
Fiber	2.5 g
Protein	19.3 g
Sodium	796 mg

* Percent Daily Values are based on a 2,000 calorie diet.

Zucchini Quiche III

Ingredients

- 6 cups grated zucchini
- 2 cups shredded Swiss cheese
- 4 eggs, beaten
- 1 cup biscuit baking mix (such as Bisquick®)
- 1/4 cup canola oil
- 1/2 tsp salt
- 1/4 tsp Italian seasoning

Directions

- Preheat your oven to 350 degrees F and put some oil over the quiche dish.
- Combine all the ingredients mentioned above thoroughly and then pour into the baking dish.
- Bake in the preheated oven for about 35 minutes or until the top of the quiche is golden brown in color.

Serving: 8

Timing Information:

Preparation	Cooking	Total Time
15 mins	35 mins	50 mins

Nutritional Information:

Calories	272 kcal
Carbohydrates	14 g
Cholesterol	107 mg
Fat	19.1 g
Fiber	1.3 g
Protein	12.2 g
Sodium	426 mg

* Percent Daily Values are based on a 2,000 calorie diet.

QUICHE QUICHE

Ingredients

- 4 eggs
- 2 cups half-and-half cream
- 1/8 tsp salt
- 1/4 tsp white pepper
- 1/8 tsp ground nutmeg
- 4 ounces Jarlsberg cheese, shredded
- 2 ounces mozzarella cheese, shredded
- 1 (9 inch pie) unbaked pie shell

Directions

- Preheat your oven to 425 degrees F and put some oil over the quiche dish.
- Whisk eggs and half-and-half until smooth in a bowl; add salt, nutmeg, and white pepper into it.
- Place shredded Jarlsberg and mozzarella in the bowl, and mix evenly before adding contents to your baking dish.

- Bake in the preheated oven for about 15 minutes and then cook for another 25 minutes at 350 degrees F or until the top of the quiche is golden brown in color.

Serving: 9

Timing Information:

Preparation	Cooking	Total Time
15 mins	30 mins	45 mins

Nutritional Information:

Calories	401 kcal
Carbohydrates	18.8 g
Cholesterol	177 mg
Fat	29.3 g
Fiber	1.1 g
Protein	15.8 g
Sodium	379 mg

* Percent Daily Values are based on a 2,000 calorie diet.

Hash Brown Quiche

Ingredients

- 1 (16 oz.) package frozen shredded hash brown potatoes, thawed
- 1/4 C. butter, melted
- 5 eggs, lightly beaten
- 1 1/2 C. shredded Swiss cheese
- 1 C. cooked ham
- 1/4 C. milk
- salt and pepper to taste

Directions

- Coat a pie dish with oil and then set your oven to 375 degrees before doing anything else.
- Fill your pie dish with the potatoes and press them down to form a crust.
- Now coat the potatoes with melted butter.
- Cook the pie dish in the oven for 17 mins.

- Now get a bowl, combine: pepper, whisked eggs, salt, milk, ham, and cheese.
- Enter this mix into the pie dish, over the potatoes, and cook the quiche in the oven for 22 more mins.
- Enjoy.

Serving: 4

Timing Information:

Preparation	Cooking	Total Time
20 m	45 m	1 h 5 m

Nutritional Information:

Calories	525 kcal
Fat	42.5 g
Carbohydrates	23.3g
Protein	27.9 g
Cholesterol	320 mg
Sodium	1722 mg

* Percent Daily Values are based on a 2,000 calorie diet.

Nutmeg and Bacon Quiche

Ingredients

- 1 (9 in.) frozen pie crust, thawed
- 1 3/4 lbs sliced bacon
- 3 eggs, lightly beaten
- 1 (12 oz.) can evaporated milk
- 1/2 tsp spicy brown mustard
- 1/4 tsp ground nutmeg
- 1/2 C. all-purpose flour, or as needed
- 1 1/2 C. shredded Swiss cheese

Directions

- Set your oven to 350 degrees before doing anything else.
- Poke some holes into your pie crust and cook it in the oven for 12 mins. Then place everything to the side.
- Now fry your bacon. And once it is crispy break it into pieces and place it to the side as well.

- Get a bowl, combine: nutmeg, whisked eggs, mustard, and milk.
- Get a 2nd bowl, combine: flour and bacon.
- Add 3/4 of the coated bacon and cheese to the pie crust then top it with the egg mix.
- Now add the rest of the bacon.
- Cook everything in the oven for 60 mins. Then let the quiche sit for 15 mins.
- Enjoy.

Serving: 8

Timing Information:

Preparation	Cooking	Total Time
15 m	1 h 15 m	1 h 40 m

Nutritional Information:

Calories	545 kcal
Fat	36.8 g
Carbohydrates	21.2g
Protein	31.2 g
Cholesterol	160 mg
Sodium	1023 mg

* Percent Daily Values are based on a 2,000 calorie diet.

Cheddar Mushroom Quiche

(Vegetarian Approved)

Ingredients

- 1 tsp salt
- 1/2 C. diced zucchini
- 1 (9 in.) unbaked pastry shell
- 2 tbsps butter
- 1 1/2 C. diced onion
- 1 green bell pepper, diced
- 1 C. diced tomatoes
- 1/2 C. sliced fresh mushrooms
- 1 clove garlic, minced
- 1/4 tsp curry powder
- 1/2 tsp salt
- 1/4 tsp ground black pepper
- 1 pin. ground cinnamon
- 5 eggs
- 1/4 C. milk
- 1/4 C. grated Parmesan cheese
- 1/4 C. shredded Cheddar cheese

Directions

- Coat your zucchini with 1 tsp of salt, in a bowl.
- Let the veggies sit in the bowl, with the salt, for 12 mins. Then remove all the resulting liquids.
- Cover a pie crust with foil and then set your oven to 450 degrees before doing anything else.
- Cook the pie crust in the oven for 6 mins, with the foil, then take off the foil, and continue cooking the crust for 6 more mins.
- Now set the oven to 350 degrees.
- Stir fry your zucchini, onion, garlic, green pepper, green pepper, mushrooms, and tomatoes for 7 mins then add: cinnamon, curry powder, pepper, and half a tsp of salt.
- Stir the contents and then pour everything into the pie crust.
- Now get a bowl, combine: cheddar, whisked eggs, parmesan, and milk.
- Pour this mix into the pie crust over the veggies.

- Cook the quiche in the oven for 50 mins. Then let it cool for 10 mins.
- Enjoy.

Serving: 6

Timing Information:

Preparation	Cooking	Total Time
30 m	55 m	1 h 40 m

Nutritional Information:

Calories	314 kcal
Fat	20.9 g
Carbohydrates	21.5g
Protein	11.2 g
Cholesterol	174 mg
Sodium	912 mg

* Percent Daily Values are based on a 2,000 calorie diet.

RUSTIC QUICHE

Ingredients

- 1/2 lb pork sausage
- 3/4 lb sliced fresh mushrooms
- 1/4 C. butter
- 2 frozen pie crusts, thawed and ready to bake
- 1 C. heavy cream
- 2 eggs, beaten
- 1 tbsp all-purpose flour
- 1 tbsp melted butter
- 1 tbsp lemon juice
- salt and pepper to taste
- 1/2 C. shredded Parmesan cheese

Directions

- Set your oven to 400 degrees before doing anything else.
- Cook your pie crust in the oven for 12 mins then set the oven's temp. to 350 degrees before doing anything else.

- Remove the pie crust from the oven.
- Stir fry your sausage until fully done and break the meat into pieces.
- Then place the sausage on some paper towel to remove the excess oils.
- Now begin to stir fry the mushrooms in butter and cook them for 7 mins.
- Combine the mushrooms and the sausage in the pie dish.
- Get a bowl, combine: pepper, cream, salt, eggs, lemon juice, flour, and butter.
- Pour this mix into your pie crust and coat everything with the parmesan.
- Place the quiche in the oven for 40 mins. Then let the contents cool for 7 mins.
- Enjoy.

Serving: 16

Timing Information:

Preparation	Cooking	Total Time
20 m	45 m	1 h 15 m

Nutritional Information:

Calories	226 kcal
Fat	18.7 g
Carbohydrates	9.6g
Protein	5.4 g
Cholesterol	63 mg
Sodium	312 mg

* Percent Daily Values are based on a 2,000 calorie diet.

SEATTLE STYLE QUICHE

Ingredients

- 1 lb fresh asparagus, trimmed and cut into 1/2 in. pieces
- 10 slices bacon
- 2 (8 in.) unbaked pie shells
- 1 egg white, lightly beaten
- 4 eggs
- 1 1/2 C. half-and-half cream
- 1/4 tsp ground nutmeg
- salt and pepper to taste
- 2 C. shredded Swiss cheese

Directions

- Set your oven to 400 degrees before doing anything else.
- Steam your asparagus, over 2 inches of boiling water, in a saucepan, using a steamer insert.
- Place a lid on the pot while the veggies steam and let them cook for 7 mins, then remove all the liquids.

- Now begin to fry your bacon until it is fully done then break it into pieces.
- Coat your pie crust with the egg whites and layer in your bacon and asparagus.
- Get a bowl, combine: pepper, eggs, salt, cream, and nutmeg.
- Pour this mix into your pie and cook everything in the oven for 37 mins.
- Enjoy.

Serving: 12

Timing Information:

Preparation	Cooking	Total Time
25 m	35 m	1 h

Nutritional Information:

Calories	334 kcal
Fat	26.3 g
Carbohydrates	12.4g
Protein	12.4 g
Cholesterol	106 mg
Sodium	383 mg

* Percent Daily Values are based on a 2,000 calorie diet.

Broccoli, Lentils, and Tomato Quiche

Ingredients

- 1 C. diced onion
- 2 tbsps olive oil
- 1/2 C. dried lentils
- 2 C. water
- 2 C. broccoli florets
- 1 C. diced fresh tomatoes
- 4 eggs, beaten
- 1 C. milk
- 1 tsp salt
- ground black pepper to taste
- 2 tsps Italian seasoning
- 1/2 C. shredded Cheddar cheese (optional)

Directions

- Set your oven to 375 degrees before doing anything else.
- Coat your pie crust with olive oil and then layer the onions in it.

- Cook the crust in the oven for 17 mins.
- Get your water and lentils boiling.
- Let the lentils cook for 22 mins. Then remove any excess liquids.
- Layer the broccoli on over the lentils and place the lid on the pot and cook the mix for 7 mins.
- Enter the tomatoes, broccoli, and lentils into the pie crust and stir the mix.
- Add the cheese as well and stir again.
- Get a bowl, combine: Italian seasoning, eggs, pepper, milk, and salt.
- Enter this mix into your pie crust as well.
- Cook everything in the oven for 50 mins then let the quiche cool for 10 mins.
- Enjoy.

Serving: 8

Timing Information:

Preparation	Cooking	Total Time
15 m	1 h 15 m	1 h 30 m

Nutritional Information:

Calories	165 kcal
Fat	9.1 g
Carbohydrates	12.4g
Protein	9.7 g
Cholesterol	103 mg
Sodium	392 mg

* Percent Daily Values are based on a 2,000 calorie diet.

Pepper and Chicken Quiche

Ingredients

- 1 (9 in.) frozen prepared pie crust, thawed
- 1 tbsp olive oil
- 1/4 C. diced onion
- 1/4 C. diced green bell pepper
- 1 tbsp all-purpose flour
- 1 C. cooked, cubed chicken meat
- 1/4 tsp salt
- 1/4 tsp ground nutmeg
- 1/4 tsp ground black pepper
- 1/2 C. shredded sharp Cheddar cheese
- 1/2 C. shredded Swiss cheese
- 2 eggs, lightly beaten
- 3/4 C. milk
- 3/4 C. sour cream

Directions

- Put your pie crust into a pie dish and then set your oven to 400 degrees before doing anything else.

- Stir fry your bell peppers and onions in olive oil for 5 mins then add the flour and continue cooking the mix for 4 mins.
- Now add the nutmeg, salt, pepper and chicken.
- Mix the contents evenly.
- Now put the chicken mix into your pie crust and place a covering of cheddar and Swiss cheese over the mix.
- Get a bowl, combine: sour cream, milk, and whisked eggs.
- Enter this mix into the pie crust as well.
- Cook the pie in the oven for 22 mins then lower the temp to 350 degrees and cook the quiche for 32 more mins.
- Enjoy.

Serving: 6

Timing Information:

Preparation	Cooking	Total Time
15 m	55 m	1 h 10 m

Nutritional Information:

Calories	389 kcal
Fat	26.5 g
Carbohydrates	19.7g
Protein	17.6 g
Cholesterol	115 mg
Sodium	454 mg

* Percent Daily Values are based on a 2,000 calorie diet.

Creamy Romano and Swiss Quiche

Ingredients

- 2 tbsps butter
- 2 C. sliced leeks
- 1 (9 in.) frozen pie crust, thawed
- 1 C. shredded Swiss cheese
- 1/4 C. grated Romano cheese
- 1 tbsp all-purpose flour
- 4 eggs
- 1 3/4 C. heavy cream
- 1 tomato, thinly sliced
- salt and pepper to taste

Directions

- Set your oven to 450 degrees before doing anything else.
- Stir fry your leeks in butter then layer them into the pie crust.
- Get a bowl, combine: flour, Romano, and Swiss. Layer these

cheeses over the veggies in the pie crust.

- Get a 2nd bowl, combine: heavy cream and whisked eggs.
- Now enter this mix into your pie crust and top everything with the pepper, salt, and tomato pieces.
- Cook everything in the oven for 16 mins then set the oven's temp to 325 degrees and cook the quiche for 27 more mins.
- Enjoy.

Serving: 8

Timing Information:

Preparation	Cooking	Total Time
15 m	45 m	1 h

Nutritional Information:

Calories	472 kcal
Fat	39.4 g
Carbohydrates	15.7g
Protein	14.9 g
Cholesterol	204 mg
Sodium	359 mg

* Percent Daily Values are based on a 2,000 calorie diet.

Artisan Sun-Dried Pesto Quiche

Ingredients

- 4 tbsps pesto
- 1 (9 in.) unbaked pie crust
- 4 tbsps crumbled goat cheese
- 3 eggs
- 1/2 C. half-and-half cream
- 1 tbsp all-purpose flour
- 8 oil-packed sun-dried tomatoes, drained and cut into strips
- salt and freshly ground black pepper to taste

Directions

- Coat your pie dish with pesto and goat cheese then set your oven to 400 degrees before doing anything else.
- Get a bowl, combine: pepper, flour, salt, cream, and whisked eggs.

- Enter this into your pie crust and then layer the sun dried tomatoes over the mix.
- Cook the quiche in the oven for 32 mins.
- Enjoy.

Serving: 8

Timing Information:

Preparation	Cooking	Total Time
15 m	30 m	45 m

Nutritional Information:

Calories	222 kcal
Fat	16.1 g
Carbohydrates	13.1g
Protein	6.6 g
Cholesterol	81 mg
Sodium	235 mg

* Percent Daily Values are based on a 2,000 calorie diet.

A QUICHE FROM MAINE

Ingredients

- 2 tbsps butter, divided
- 1/4 C. plain dried bread crumbs
- 2 C. 2% milk
- 8 oz. salmon fillets, skin removed
- 1/3 C. diced onion
- 1/2 bunch Swiss chard, diced
- 1/2 tsp salt
- 1/8 tsp ground black pepper
- 1/2 tsp dried marjoram
- 1/8 tsp ground nutmeg
- 3 eggs

Directions

- Coat a pie dish with 1 tbsp of butter then set your oven to 350 degrees before doing anything else.
- Now coat the pie dish with bread crumbs and shake off any excess.
- Begin to simmer your salmon in milk, in a large pot with a lid.

- Cook the salmon for 12 mins.
- Now in a separate pan begin to stir fry your chards and onions in the rest of the butter.
- Once all of the liquid has cooked out add: nutmeg, salt, marjoram, and pepper.
- Remove everything from the pan and let the contents cool.
- Enter the onion mix in to the pie dish and then flake your salmon into the mix as well.
- Now get a bowl, combine: 1 C. of milk from the salmon and the eggs.
- Pour this into the pie crust as well and cook everything in the oven for 40 mins.
- Enjoy.

Serving: 8

Timing Information:

Preparation	Cooking	Total Time
45 m	35 m	1 h 20 m

Nutritional Information:

Calories	154 kcal
Fat	9.3 g
Carbohydrates	6.7g
Protein	10.8 g
Cholesterol	99 mg
Sodium	289 mg

* Percent Daily Values are based on a 2,000 calorie diet.

Cherry Tomatoes and Kale Quiche

Ingredients

- 1 C. diced kale
- 1 small leek, white and light green parts only, sliced
- 4 oz. halved cherry tomatoes
- 4 eggs
- 1 C. milk
- 4 oz. shredded Italian cheese blend
- 1 sprig fresh rosemary, finely diced
- 1 pin. sea salt
- 1/8 tsp ground black pepper
- 1 tbsp grated Parmesan cheese

Directions

- Coat a pie plate with oil and then set your oven to 375 degrees before doing anything else.

- Steam your kale over 2 inches of boiling water, in a large pot, using a steamer insert.
- Place a lid on the pot and let the contents cook for 7 mins. Then place the kale into the pie plate.
- Now combine the sliced tomatoes and leeks with the kale.
- Get a bowl, combine: black pepper, milk, sea salt, cheese, and rosemary.
- Enter this mix into the pie plate and stir the contents.
- Cook everything in the oven for 35 mins.
- Now place a topping of parmesan over the quiche and continue cooking it in the oven for 15 more mins.
- Enjoy.

Serving: 8

Timing Information:

Preparation	Cooking	Total Time
15 m	55 m	1 h 10 m

Nutritional Information:

Calories	110 kcal
Fat	7 g
Carbohydrates	4.1g
Protein	8 g
Cholesterol	106 mg
Sodium	217 mg

* Percent Daily Values are based on a 2,000 calorie diet.

Nutty Honey Quiche

Ingredients

- 1/2 C. butter
- 1 C. sliced carrots
- 1 C. cashews
- 1/2 C. honey
- 3 eggs
- 1 1/2 C. heavy cream
- 1/2 tsp nutmeg
- 1/2 tsp salt
- 3/4 C. shredded Cheddar cheese
- 1 (9 in.) pie crust

Directions

- Set your oven to 350 degrees before doing anything else.
- Stir fry your cashews and carrots in melted butter until the carrots are soft.
- Now add in your honey, stir the mix, and shut the heat.
- Get a bowl, combine: salt, eggs, nutmeg, and heavy cream.

- Layer your cheese into the pie dish and then place the cashew mix on top before pouring in the cream mix.
- Cook everything in the oven for 38 mins.
- Enjoy.

Serving: 8

Timing Information:

Preparation	Cooking	Total Time
20 m	40 m	1 h

Nutritional Information:

Calories	586 kcal
Fat	47.4 g
Carbohydrates	34.1g
Protein	10.2 g
Cholesterol	175 mg
Sodium	468 mg

* Percent Daily Values are based on a 2,000 calorie diet.

NUTTY TANGY CHICKEN QUICHE

Ingredients

- 1 C. diced, cooked chicken
- 1 C. shredded Swiss cheese
- 1/4 C. diced onion
- 1 tbsp all-purpose flour
- 1/2 C. diced pecans
- 1 (9 in.) unbaked deep-dish pastry shell
- 2 eggs, beaten
- 1 C. 2% milk
- 1/2 tsp brown mustard

Directions

- Set your oven to 325 degrees before doing anything else.
- Get a bowl, combine: 1/4 C. pecans, chicken, flour, cheese, and onions. Enter this into your pie.
- Get a 2nd bowl, combine: mustard, the rest of the pecans,

milk, and eggs. Layer this mix over the chicken mix in the pie crust and cook everything in the oven for 55 mins.

- Enjoy.

Serving: 8

Timing Information:

Preparation	Cooking	Total Time
20 m	50 m	1 h 10 m

Nutritional Information:

Calories	339 kcal
Fat	23 g
Carbohydrates	15.5g
Protein	18 g
Cholesterol	92 mg
Sodium	237 mg

* Percent Daily Values are based on a 2,000 calorie diet.

Mexican Style Quiche

Ingredients

- 1 (9 in.) unbaked deep-dish pie crust
- 10 oz. chorizo sausage
- 6 eggs
- 1/4 C. milk
- 1 (10 oz.) can diced tomatoes with green chili peppers (such as RO*TEL(R)), drained
- 2 C. shredded Mexican cheese blend, divided
- 1 (15 oz.) can refried beans

Directions

- Layer your pie crust into a pie dish and then set your oven to 400 degrees before doing anything else.
- Stir fry your chorizo for 7 mins then break it into pieces.
- Get a bowl, combine: milk and eggs. Then add in half of the

cheese, the chili pepper, and the tomatoes. Stir everything together.

- Layer your beans into the pie crust and evenly distribute them.
- Now add in the chorizo and the egg mix. Top the quiche with the rest of the cheese.
- Cook the quiche in the oven for 50 mins.
- Enjoy.

Serving: 8

Timing Information:

Preparation	Cooking	Total Time
15 m	50 m	1 h 20 m

Nutritional Information:

Calories	520 kcal
Fat	36.4 g
Carbohydrates	23.1g
Protein	25.2 g
Cholesterol	208 mg
Sodium	1196 mg

* Percent Daily Values are based on a 2,000 calorie diet.

ARTISAN STYLE SPINACH QUICHE

Ingredients

- 1 (9 in.) unbaked pie crust
- 4 eggs
- 5 slices cooked bacon, crumbled
- 1/2 C. shredded mozzarella cheese
- 2 tbsps milk
- 2 tbsps all-purpose flour
- 2 cloves garlic, minced
- 1 tsp parsley
- 1/2 tsp thyme
- 1 C. spinach leaves, divided
- 1/2 C. canned artichoke hearts, drained and diced
- 2 roma (plum) tomatoes, sliced

Directions

- Layer your pie crust into the pie plate then set your oven to 350 degrees before doing anything else.

- Get a bowl, combine: thyme, eggs, parsley, bacon, garlic, mozzarella, flour, and milk.
- Layer half of your spinach into the crust then add the artichokes on top.
- Enter in the milk mix and then layer the tomato pieces on top of everything.
- Cook the quiche in the oven for 50 mins.
- Enjoy.

Serving: 6

Timing Information:

Preparation	Cooking	Total Time
15 m	45 m	1 h

Nutritional Information:

Calories	274 kcal
Fat	17.1 g
Carbohydrates	19g
Protein	11.4 g
Cholesterol	136 mg
Sodium	442 mg

* Percent Daily Values are based on a 2,000 calorie diet.

THANKS FOR READING! NOW LET'S TRY SOME **SUSHI** AND **DUMP DINNERS**....

Send the Book!

To grab this **box set** simply follow the link mentioned above, or tap the book cover.

This will take you to a page where you can simply enter your email address and a PDF version of the **box set** will be emailed to you.

I hope you are ready for some serious cooking!

Send the Book!

You will also receive updates about all my new books when they are free.

Also don't forget to like and subscribe on the social networks. I love meeting my readers. Links to all my profiles are below so please click and connect :)

Facebook

Twitter

COME ON...
LET'S BE FRIENDS :)

I adore my readers and love connecting with them socially. Please follow the links below so we can connect on Facebook, Twitter, and Google+.

Facebook

Twitter

I also have a blog that I regularly update for my readers so check it out below.

My Blog

About The Publisher.

BookSumo specializes in providing the best books on special topics that you care about. The *Easy Quiche Cookbook* will demystify this complex dish for the novice chef and the expert chef alike!

To find out more about BookSumo and find other books we have written go to:

http://booksumo.com/.

CAN I ASK A FAVOUR?

If you found this book interesting, or have otherwise found any benefit in it. Then may I ask that you post a review of it on Amazon? Nothing excites me more than new reviews, especially reviews which suggest new topics for writing. I do read all reviews and I always factor feedback into my newer works.

So if you are willing to take ten minutes to write what you sincerely thought about this book then please visit our Amazon page and post your opinions.

Again thank you!

INTERESTED IN OTHER EASY COOKBOOKS?

Everything is easy! Check out my Amazon Author page for more great cookbooks:

For a complete listing of all my books please see my author page.

25610464R00090

Printed in Great Britain
by Amazon